Compassion at the Cross

Author:
Ova Mae English

Published by:
Lisa Dziedzic

Illustrations by:
Lisa Dziedzic
Emily Dziedzic

ISBN: Paperback 979-8-9895002-0-8
ISBN: E-Book 979-8-9895002-1-5
ISBN: Hardcover 979-8-9895002-2-2

Dedication

This publication is dedicated to my children as a partial compilation of their great-grandmother's poetry written over her lifetime. It encompasses a spiritual view and observations of experiences as a Christian woman living through poverty, multiple wars, and life experiences throughout the 1900's.

I hope you enjoy it as much I have while editing and illustrating this journey.

Lisa Dziedzic

Contents

INTRODUCTION

My poems are a hodgepodge
of sunshine and of rain,
of joy and laughter
or sometimes of pain.

Some speak of contentment
which I strive to attain,
some are a bit funny
some quite inane.

Oft, they are praise
to the father above,
for the wonderful gift
of his mercy and love.

Or thanks for guiding
my steps each day
that I may not stumble
or fall by the way.

Some speak of hope
for a much brighter day
when all sounds of man's warring
and strife have passed away.

Some are just an expression
of a deep and heartfelt prayer
that all men know of God's coming Kingdom,
that they may, its blessings share.

SEEKING HIS SHEEP

I hear folks talk about the Shepherd
who seeks His sheep that stray,
upon some lonely desert
or on a mountain, cold and gray.

Then I hear them talk about the Church
His body, they all say,
while He is up in heaven
awaiting that great day.

As I sit and ponder
one thing becomes quite clear,
if I'm His feet, why am I not walking,
and seeking, far and near?

If I'm His eyes, I should be looking
or His hands reach out to live,
some lamb, so cold and frightened
that from the fold did drift.

If I'm His voice, I hear no echo
from each crag, so loud and clear,
a sound to give direction
to His lost sheep everywhere.

If I'm His heart
my compassion and love should not be bound,
for me, there'd be no resting
'til the last sheep had been found.

Forgive me Blessed Shepherd
I'm glad you found me here today,
it seems I must have drifted
from the flock and lost my way.

GOD'S HAND

I see God's hand in everything
that lives or moves or grows,
from the smallest of his creatures
to a fragrant, full-grown rose.

I see Him in the hazy mists
that veil the mountain tall,
in the glowing hour of sunset
and the colors rich of Fall.

I hear Him in the thunder
that bursts across the sky,
in the song of a happy robin
from His nesting place nearby.

I hear Him in the cricket's call
and buzzing of the bees,
the quiet rustle of the wind
whispering through the trees.

I feel Him in a ray sunshine
on a dark and gloomy day,
in the soft and gentle breezes
that around my face doth play.

I feel His presence near me
His love embraces all,
He knows my every struggle
He even notes the sparrow's fall.

When sorrow's clouds surround me
and the dark becomes my day,
He sends His blessed sunshine
to drive my clouds away.

I know that He is living
whatever ills betide,
and that He's ne'er so far away
those clouds His face can hide.

GOD THE WORTHY JUDGE

You, who would judge another,
is your robe quite clean and white,
or have you perhaps forgotten
to view it in the light?

You, who brand others foolish
or inferior of mind,
have you searched your own so closely
and failed one flaw to find?

You, whose zeal for fighting Satan
is uprooting tares so neat,
are you sure that you have done it
without rooting up the wheat?

God needs teachers true and patient
with his love in heart and mind,
but He alone is fitted
to be Judge of all mankind.

BE STILL AND KNOW

In quietness and peace
thy strength shall ever be,
the tumult and the shouting
are for others not for Thee.

My rod shall be thy comfort
thou shalt feed in pastures green,
and the wonders I will show Thee
other eyes have seldom seen.

By swift waters I will lead Thee
in a path where all have trod,
who have heard my gentle voice
be still and know that I am God.

*The religion of Jesus Christ
is neither noise or silence,
but a way of life.*

THE GREATEST OF THE GREATEST

Born of kingly lineage,
a manger for a bed,
sent from heaven's portal
no pillow for his head.

Oft' foretold by prophets,
this long awaited one,
He was the greatest of the greatest
God's own beloved Son.

He was a man of sorrow
who walked earth's paths alone,
condemned and oft' rejected
by those He called his own.

The perfect lamb,
a sacrifice, from sin to set us free,
He was the greatest of the greatest
He died for you and me.

Oft' He healed man's sickness
and caused their eyes to see,
yet they even spat upon him
and nailed him to a tree.

The tomb? It could not hold him,
He won the victory,
He was the greatest of the greatest,
He conquered death for you and me.

He ascended up to heaven,
but He's coming back we're told,
this time in kingly splendor
as the prophets said of old

To bind the powers of Satan
and at last to set men free,
He is the greatest of the greatest
and ever more shall be.

MY MORNING PRAYER

Give to me your grace, dear Lord
to greet each dawning day,
with a calm and quiet spirit
for its problems come what may.

Let me see possibilities
for each task that lies ahead,
rather than thoughts of failure
that bring only fear and dread.

Let me feel your leading
as each coming hour I view,
that I may only see them
as a challenge fresh and new.

That when the day is over
I may look back with thankful heart,
and only feel a spirit
as serene as at the start.

WHEN THE TRUMPET SOUNDS

When the trumpet sounds its message
echoing o'er land and sea,
heralding the day of judgment
where men may be.

When at last the Lord shall call you
for reward or sins to pay,
when you face him in the judgment
this is what you'll hear him say.

Did you ever love your brother
help him in his time of need?
Did you clothe the cold and naked
or the hungry, did you feed?

Did you heed the way I taught you?
When on earth I walked and then,
Did you help to build my kingdom
in the minds of hearts of men?

There will be no need to answer
in the book of life my friend,
and the words that you have written
and by these you'll be condemned.

Or your heart will sing for gladness
as you know the victory's won,
when you hear, WELL DONE thou faithful
enter into life My son.

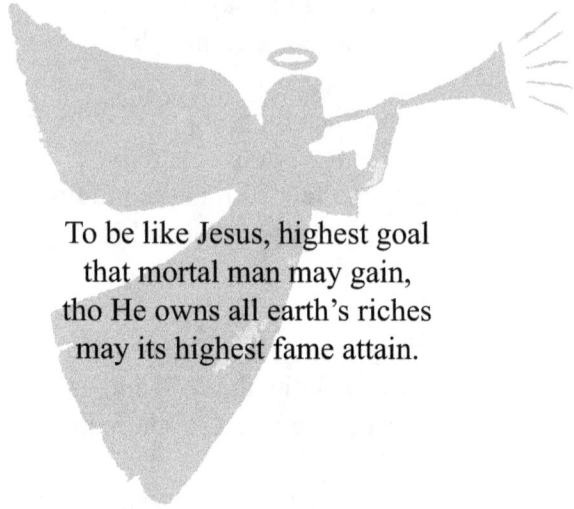

To be like Jesus, highest goal
that mortal man may gain,
tho He owns all earth's riches
may its highest fame attain.

GOD IS MY REFUGE

God is my refuge and my strength,
through all the stormy blasts,
His hand shall ever guide me
'til time on earth is past.

When I shall reach that river,
face the ebbing of the tide,
His hand it still shall guide me
'til I reach the other side.

Then on through life eternal
where I never more shall die,
His hand it still shall guide me
as the years flow swiftly by.

IN HIS FOOTSTEPS

What does it mean to walk in the steps
of that man from Galilee?
What does it mean to follow
in the path He set for me?

In that straight and narrow pathway
leading ever upward each day,
'til I reach that golden portal
at the end of life's rugged way.

He loved enough to give His life
at a hill called Calvary,
His blood flowed down to erase the sins
of one so unworthy as me.

He extended a hand of mercy
to those who were so distressed,
to those who were worn and weary
He offered a haven of rest.

He often spoke words of comfort
that brought healing to hearts and minds,
And to follow in His footsteps
I must echo those deeds in kind.

PRAISE AND THANKSGIVING

Some folks pray for many things
of gold or stone or brass,
for earthly power or prestige
for fame that soon shall pass.

But this is all I pray
for when Lord I come to Thee,
a time to praise and thank Thee
for all Thou givest me.

A task that I may labor
in every way I can,
to bring Thy Kingdom nearer
to the heart of every man.

Thy tender hand to lead me
Thy love my light to be,
and the wondrous, sweet assurance
I'll be ever nigh to Thee.

THE HOUR OF DELIVERANCE

Row on row the shadows
have encompassed us about,
while ever howling o'er us
are the winds of fear and doubt.

Evil forces have enmeshed us
with their bitterness and hate,
and it often seems the clamor
of war and strife will n'er abate.

Yet the lengthening of the shadows
stretching forth across the land,
prove the hour of deliverance
is now so near at hand.

That in spite of all the evil
the wicked one can bring,
we can lift our heart in gladness
to look up and laugh and sing.

GOD, MY GUIDE

God is the compass, and faith the light,
that guides my ship through the darkest night.

I'd only be lost and helpless so torn by fear and doubt,
in the midst of life's angry current if these I sailed without.

I'd drift o'er a course uncharted through a sea all flecked with foam,
'til I at last was dashed to pieces far from the shores of home.

Lord, take my life and let it be,
a channel of love sent forth from Thee,
let me give it to others who come my way
to lift their burden, and brighten their day.

BEYOND THE TOMB

So oft' I hear of darkness
and the closing of the day,
so oft' I hear of sunset
and the ending of the way.

Of a valley dim with shadows
that we all must walk alone,
of a life that fast if fleeting
that will soon be o'er and gone.

Yet, when my friends would warn me
of a doom fast drawing near,
of an event that is approaching
of a time to greatly fear.

I point them to the Master
and the stone He rolled away,
to the light that glows beyond it
heralding a brighter day.

I see no sun, fast sinking,
for I face the eastern sky,
my life is just beginning
and the dawn, at last is nigh.

This is just a preparation
for the years that are to be,
when the Lord's "well done"
is spoken and His glory I shall see.

Death is just a doorway
that one day swung open wide,
when my Lord its portal entered
and its fetters there untied.

Death's chain could never hold Him
soon He came forth, glad and free,
And I hear His joyful message
as it echoes back to me.

Death never more can claim you
if in Me you do believe,
I have paid for you a ransom
and your fears I will relieve

So I labor here with patience
'til the shadows all shall flee,
As I sail out with the sunrise
into life's eternity.

MY TESTIMONY

If I ever tried to tell you all the Lord for me has done,
after I had talked a hundred years, I would have only just begun.

To tell of times He comforted, gave help in times of need,
or of when I walked in darkness and I felt His spirit lead.

Of how my prayers were answered when I did his blessing seek
or how His strength sustained me when I was weary, worn and weak.

Of how I'm never lonely because I know He's always there,
waiting to hear my song of joy or my greatest sorrow share.

Or even if I've fallen to lift me up you see,
to heal my broken spirit and wrap my wounded knee.

Although I can't see the future, I have no pangs of fear or dread,
for knowing that He's leading and knows what lies ahead.

JOYS OF THE NEW EARTH

There's a great day coming
when man shall weep no more,
when the earth is filled with gladness
and shall sing from shore to shore.

For the great Redeemer cometh
King of Kings from heaven is He,
to bind the powers of Satan
and at last to set men free.

Every tongue shall confess Him
every head hang down in shame,
that did no give Him honor
or lift up His holy name.

Every knee shall bow before Him
and acknowledge He is King
and the earth shall ever after
with His joyful praises ring.

THE COMFORTER'S VOICE

I walked among the shadows
and lo! My Lord was there,
to whisper words of comfort
and dry my bitter tear.

When the night was over
the shadows did depart,
I walked out in the sunshine
a song within my heart.

Then soft across the morning
came a voice so kind and true,
if you truly would be happy
let Me share your gladness too!

ASSURANCE

Sometimes my thoughts are wild and free
as a bird in swift soaring flight,
sometimes they are quiet and gentle
as when day blends into the night.

Sometimes they cause a deep heartache
for a world filled with strife and much pain,
for the people whose leaders think only
of the way to more power or gain.

And then they rise upward on wings of great joy
and God's peace supreme fills my heart,
for I know the Creator is yet in command
just as He was at the start.

That nothing that Satan can ever devise
can alter or change it one whit,
but that all of His plan will be carried out
according to His holy writ.

THE LORD IS MY SHEPHERD

The Lord is my shepherd,
my strength, my hope, my joy,
He's the one I can depend on
when the cares of life annoy.

I have hope that springs eternal
tho my skies so dark may be,
for I have His light to guide me
that I may fully see.

He's the rock of my salvation,
He's the pilot of my life,
He gives me peace and comfort
in the midst of pain and strife.

Just to know He walks beside me
and His strength is at my command,
gives me all the confidence
I need to walk this weary land.

IF THERE WERE NO EYES

All the wonders of the universe would nevermore be viewed,
or the rich and myriad beauty with which our planet is endued.

God made eyes to view the heavens on a starlit summer night,
or to see a rosy sunset by the evening's fading light.

God made eyes to watch the flutter of a lazy butterfly's wing,
as it searches for some nectar in the early days of Spring.

God made eyes to watch the antics of a happy carefree child,
or to watch two kittens frolic in a setting, free and wild.

God made eyes to see the love light in the face of someone dear,
or to view it with compassion when it sheds a bitter tear.

God made eyes to see the splendor of his creation, great and fair,
that we may know of His great caring by the home He did prepare.

If there were no eyes, I quietly ponder, beauty, abundant rich & free,
Forever would be wasted if there were no eyes to see.

WE ARE THE TEMPLE

I was reading a psalm written long ago
by a man with a heart, grieved and sore,
because the enemies of God
seemed bolder than ever before.

They scorned God's people
wherever they came,
they denied His power
and mocked His name.

Ane he cried how long, O Lord
how long, will you silent be,
while they criticize freely
and make fun of Thee.

And I thought of conditions
that are the same today,
just as they were
in that time, far away.

Why don't we speak up
and His honor defend,
and these lies and this subterfuge
bring to an end.

Then in my mind
a voice rang clear,
just as though someone
was standing near.

Don't you know My child?
I have no choice,
you are My tongue,
My lips, My voice.

You are My temple
in which I dwell,
yours is the voice
that My wonders tell.

Then I wept, how long, O Lord,
How long will we silent be?
How long 'til we arise
and speak up for Thee?

Against the evil forces
that abound on every hand,
throughout the length
and the breadth of this land.

As they seek to destroy
Thy word and power,
just as they did
in that long-gone hour.

FOR EVIL – FOR GOOD

Once in a manger, crude and so low,
a tiny babe slept 'neath the moon's silver glow.

A nation stirred in slumber and gave a soft sigh,
never knowing that her hour of decision was nigh.

Only some shepherds that night on a hill,
heard the heavenly message of peace and good will.

Only some wise men in a nation afar,
watched the broad heavens to follow His star.

The babe grew to manhood taught year after year,
watching her indifference with a grief-stricken tear.

She spurned all of His teachings raised up the cross high,
decreeing that God's own Beloved should die.

With violence and hate, she sated her lust,
while her once proud destiny crumbled to dust.

Swift came her judgment as armies marched nigh,
battering and crushing her many walls, high.

Blood flowed as a river in her streets they say,
as her hour of decision passed swiftly away.

Fast flowed the years of the centuries by,
while many great empires arose, but to die.

Brought down by decision spurred by men's lust,
until their lone marker is ashes and dust.

The hour fast approaches, draws ever more near,
when man must decide his last destiny here.

All of his dreams could mount up to the sky,
or hope fold her mantle to wither and die.

The hour of decision hangs heavy today,
while war clouds are gathering o'er our word, cold and gray.

The torch of hope which once burned so hith,
is now but a glimmer against the dark sky.

Yet God has placed in our hand a chalice of gold,
whose content could bring blessing to all people untold.

It could banish man's want, cure his many grave ills,
but "nay" quote the tempter, we shall use it to kill.

Blend it with hate and a great lust for power,
that man may drink deep in his last tragic hour.

O'er the tumult, the words of the Master ring clear,
use it to banish earth's want and her fear.

Use all of its power to bring nigh the day,
when man shall find joy in a quiet, peaceful way.

For evil? For good? God help us we pray,
ere our hour of decision pass swiftly away.

Written at the advent of atomic energy.
The answer.....only time will tell.

THE GREATNESS OF GOD

How great my friend is the God you serve?
How powerful? How strong?
Can He smooth the path before you
change your sorrow into song?

Can He lift you when you've fallen?
soothe your spirit, bruised and sore?
with whispered words of comfort,
can He do all this and more?

Can He give you peace within your heart?
Can He joy in fullness bring?
until deep down within your heart
you can hear the joybells ring.

Did he die to pay your ransom
because He loved you so?
Did He rise again in glory
that your eternal life might know?

If your God is weak and helpless
when the storm is raging nigh,
if he has no power to save you
when the waves come dashing high.

Then come and I will show you
a place to anchor deep,
where through all the storms of life
your bark will safely keep.

Tis my great God eternal
ever living, ever true
nothing on earth or heaven
beyond His power can do.

WALK AMONG THE SHADOWS

Oh! Toiling masses of humanity
forever seeking, groping,
to rise above the shadows
for surer life, e'er hoping.

'Tis Christ you seek, the promised one
proclaimed in song and story,
'tis He alone can lift you up,
high o'er your gloom and sorrow
to walk above the shadows
in a glorious, bright tomorrow.

No burden is too heavy
if you are by my side,
but joy would lose its meaning
if my sins your face did hide.

A LIGHTENED LOAD

I carried a load that was heavy
I even felt bent 'neath its weight,
I stumbled along on the pathway
although it was even and straight.

Why do you carry this burden?
a voice spoke soft in my ear,
Why is your heart filled with sadness?
Why all this worry and care?

Don't you know for all of your weakness,
I have strength enough to spare?
Don't you know I have felt the same heartache
and known the same worries and cares.

I know when the sparrow is falling,
whether evening, nighttime or day,
I know although darkness surround you,
what's around the next bend in the way.

Let me have your life and its problems
give me your worries and fears,
I'll give you joy for your sorrows
and laughter for all of your tears.

In Me, you'll find quiet contentment
the peace that I only can give,
and at last you will know life's full meaning
as you begin to abundantly live.

ALL ON THE ALTAR

I thought my Lord required
I give all that I did possess,
a tenth so I in duty
gave a tenth and not one whit less.

I thought the other was mine alone
to buy what I wished or be lent
not knowing that He would take account
of how or why it was spent.

I thought the way was of duty
of burden and sacrifice,
the Kingdom of God was only
for those that would pay the price.

Then one day my Master called me.
I answered, here, Lord am I,
lead and I will follow,
though the way be lowly or high.

Then He opened a way before me
that glowed with mercy and love,
the eyes that one had been blinded
He filled with light from above.

My heart that had known only duty
was touched by burdens and care,
of others that dwelt about me
with their toil, their trouble and fear.

Now when my Savior calls me,
my brother, my priest, my friend,
I joyfully walk beside Him
and help His sheep to tend.

No more is our life divided
by a tenth and not one whit less
But we gladly use together
all that we do possess.

THE MASTER'S WAY

Whenever you are tempted
to turn your feet away,
from the path that God doth lead you
where you know he bids you stay.

Whenever you're discouraged,
your patience sorely tried,
because everyone doth question
and from your teaching turn aside.

Then turn your thoughts to Jesus
how they scorned him day by day,
how they mocked and called him
foolish to teach such humble way.

How the Pharisees, so haughty
their head held high in price,
With their many tricky questions
His spirit sorely tired.

Yet, he calmly gave them answer,
walked with patience day by day,
ever giving help and comfort
to those along His way.

Teaching truth so long forgotten
'neath tradition's sullen tide,
while few would hear His message
or 'neath its banner hide.

Know ye not that in our church's tradition
yet o'er men holds sway,
and few will hear your message
if you teach the Master's way.

THE JUDGMENT

Now is the judgment of this world
the prince shall be cast,
thus spoke the Master long ago
so why should men still doubt?

And follow ways of evil
when full well they know,
each has his hour of judgment
by the way he chooses to go.

When He shall cast out Satan
those today who choose His way,
must follow in His judgment
on that great and final day.

GOD'S PLAN

The law of God is simple
and plain as it can be,
tho we often try to make it hard
for other folks to see.

We may search through all the scriptures
citing rules from A to Z,
but when we reach the final truth
He only gave us three.

Thou shall love the Lord thy God
with all thy heart and mind,
as thou dost love thyself,
thy neighbor, love in kind.

The third law comes from Jesus,
humble man of Galilee,
Thou shalt love thy Christian brother
as much as I have love for thee.

On these laws, unchanged, unchanging,
hang all God's will for man,
and we question His wise judgment
when we try to change His plan.

A PRAYER FOR STRENGTH

Teach me O Lord eternal
to humbly walk each day,
as thou once walked so long ago
within the narrow way.

To speak no word but truth
Dear Lord, give me Thy courage true,
for Lord, I have no strength
but Thine to aid Thy will to do.

I thank you for each blessing
That you send from day to day,
to help me bear my burdens
as I travel on life's way.

I do not ask a lighter load or paths
that are smooth and fair,
just grant me strength from day to day
to aid my cross to bear.

FAITHFUL SERVICE

I came to my Lord in sorrow,
to repent of my sin and shame,
to ask him to forgive me,
to trust in His holy name.

Then as I knelt before him,
go forth at once quoth He,
bring fruits that are meant,
for repentance and pardon, I'll give to Thee.

For all who repent before me
must prove that they are sincere,
if you truly seek forgiveness,
you must serve me faithfully here.

SEEK AND YOU SHALL FIND

So long I sought the Master in earth's many faiths and creeds,
yet in them all, I found not one that satisfied my needs.

There was always something lacking, they could not open the door
that seemed fast closed, upon the light of truth forevermore.

One said" My way's the only way, just come and walk with me,"
Another said, "Oh no, you're wrong, for only my way's right you
see."

In my mind, there reigned confusion and at last a dark despair,
it made my spirit bow in grief so deep, I scarce the load could bear.

Then as I meditated, at last there came a light,
a faint and far off glimmer thro' the darkness of the night.

On swift wings my spirit found it and the Master's words came thro',
only to the humble will I give the message true.

To those who never love me, heed the way that once I taught,
who follow in my footsteps in word and deed and thought.

Who walk with hand extended as a friend to all in need,
who never stop to question either color, race, or creed.

I know no creed or color, notoriety or fame,
but give My spirit freely to all who call upon My name.

I prayed: I thank Thee Master, thou indeed hast set me free,
and he answered, O so gently, and lo; I abide with Thee.

A WASTED LIFE

If I could live on this earth for a thousand years,
amid all of its conflicts, it joys, and its fears.

And I never did anything but idle away,
the time that God gave me to work and to play.

If I never gave anyone a helping hand,
or lifted his burden that he might stand.

If I never gave the message from His Holy Word,
to some lonely person that had never heard.

If all that I said or I did was to give pleasure to me,
with no thought of a tomorrow that was to be.

When the books were balanced with figures quite true,
there would be no record that I had ever passed through.

LET ME DWELL BESIDE YOU

I want no house your hands have built,
so cold and bleak and bare,
where I must sit alone and wait
for you to seek Me there.

Just let Me dwell within your home
where warmth and love abound,
where friendly talk and laughter
bind hearts the circle round.

I would share your hour of labor
and your fun and playtime too,
I would be a kind companion
a friend that's tried and true.

Build your house of worship
where together you may pray,
but let Me dwell beside you
to bless you every day.

GOD'S LAW ALONE IS PERFECT

My child, teach not man's word or his wisdom
teach not the rules that he gives,
teach only My truth, undiluted
the words by which man dies or lives.

Man's rules are so imperfect
with such human error fraught,
for naught but dust has made them
in their words no wisdom wrought.

My law alone is perfect
crystal clear defining sin,
so plain and very simple
even fools err not therein.

WHY DID YOU NOT ANSWER?

Once Jesus called in Galilee
in days that long are past,
for laborers in his harvest,
that then was ripening fast.

The precious grain is wasting
there is much work to do,
Can't you hear me calling,
calling now for you?

He's called down through the ages
as He called back then,
Will you for Me labor
again and once again?

The fields are white to harvest
the laborers are so few,
Can't you hear me calling,
calling now for you?

Laborers for the harvest
the Master calls today,
the wages are eternal life
at the ending of the way.

The fields are all ripened
the laborers are so few,
Can't you hear me calling,
calling now for you?

The night is now approaching
soon harvest will be past,
no more time to labor
and we'll hear his voice at last.

The fields were white to harvest,
the laborers were so few,
Why? Oh Why, did you not answer
when I called for you?

A BIBLE VIEW OF JESUS

When I view the pictures that the many artists paint,
of a man so very handsome and quite effeminate.

And they say it looks like Jesus when He walked on earth with men,
I sure would like to tell them, you'll just have to try again.

If I could paint great pictures as the famous artists do,
I'd like to paint him from the Bible and then compare the two.

I'd pain hands to hold a hammer, erect a structure built so true,
it would outlast all of the efforts that the best of men might do.

I'd paint him standing straight with shoulders broad and strong,
as when He cleansed the temple of its merchandising throng.

I'd paint his eyes so piercing that He could even see,
a man like small Zacchaeus, hidden way up in a tree.

I'd paint Him like an athlete, all bronzed, by wind and sun,
as He received the victor's crown when at last the race was won.

I know He looks much different now up near the throne of God,
but this is how the Bible paints Him on the paths of earth He trod.

HEAVEN TO ME

Some say God's kingdom is a place whose streets are purest gold,
that He has built above the stars with mansions fair untold.

Where His children all shall go, a robe and crown to wear,
and only sing and shout and forever stay up there.

Yet others say 'tis here below His kingdom He has planned,
to start the golden age of peace and evermore to stand.

That Satan ever shall be bound and every man be free,
to build a life of happiness in true security.

I care not if tis up above in some galaxy far,
revolving 'round another sun, a bright and shining star.

Or if 'tis just on earth below that heaven may be found,
when I shall rise immortal, no more by death's chain bound.

For this I know within my heart, God dwells today and so,
I know that He'll be with me wherever I may go.

And if 'tis here or far away on some remotest star,
to be with Him is heaven, 'tho it be near or far.

GOD'S DECREE

East is east and west is west
but they shall join together,
love's cord of gold shall bind their hearts
forever and forever.

'Tis God's decree so who will dare
to criticize or question,
the edict of Him who knows
the whys of all creation.

GOD STILL IS LOVE

God made man in His own image
in the ages long ago,
and his life was filled with sunshine
of His presence here below.

God walked with him each morning
and talked with him each night,
as they wandered in the garden
by the evening's fading light.

Then the wicked one sowed evil
that sprang up as hate and greed,
changing man from God's own image
with this rank and ugly weed.

Where love's blossom bloomed in beauty,
sweet its fragrance on the air,
now this weed is growing rampant
choking out its beauty there.

Oh! That man might see the vision,
see how futile is his life,
cast out Satan's ugly harvest
of hate, and greed, and strife.

Let love's blossom grow and flourish
as in ages long ago,
when man was in His image
for God still is love, you know.

GOD'S KINGDOM

I seek a kingdom ruled by God,
a world that has no night,
for so I learn from His own book
His word shall be the light.

That guides all people here
that dwell within His realm so fair,
and grief and pain and sorrow
shall never enter there.

All men shall dwell forever
there upheld by God's own hand,
in perfect peace and happiness
within a perfect land.

THE MOCKINGBIRD SONG

I saw a mockingbird today
upon a tree branch high,
a small and very common bird
outlined against the sky.

It seemed pure joy was pouring forth
with each note, clear and sweet,
joy so great it even
reached his tiny little feet.

Many times, he spread his wings
and rose as if to fly,
then came back down to rest again
upon that tree branch, high.

A never once he missed a note
nor faltered in his song,
I wondered how such happiness
could to one small bird belong.

AFTER THE RAIN

There is nothing quite so wondrous
as a rain-drenched summer day,
after the storm is over
and the clouds have rolled away.

A fragrant, clean aroma
from each tree, plant and flower,
fills the earth with the sweetest fragrance
in this rain-washed hour.

As rays of golden sunshine,
the mists come peeping through,
To create a shining rainbow crown
for a world that's fresh and new.

MY PRAYER FOR YOU

That God will grant you success in whatever you choose to do,
you'll let His hand e'er guide you and light the path for you.

That you'll learn that seeking fortune in earthly wealth or fame,
is not the road to happiness your heart seeks to attain.

Many, although wealthy, have problems worse than you,
with thoughts of thieves and robbers, sometimes of kidnappers too.

Many, although famous, along the fast lanes go,
caught up in drugs and alcohol, and only misery know.

That you'll learn some words of kindness spoken even to a foe,
will light the torch of friendship wherever you may go.

That just loving, selfless giving, with no reward in mind,
will bring you all the happiness you'll ever need to find.

Written for our youth as they venture out into the world.

A LOSING BATTLE

We fight the battle of the sag
as the years go passing by,
and we never seem to wind one,
no matter how we try.

For gravity, that magic force
that holds us on the ground,
and keeps us anchored firm and sure
so we can't float around.

Just keeps on pulling, tugging
and never once does cease,
I guess we should just give it up
and spend our life in peace.

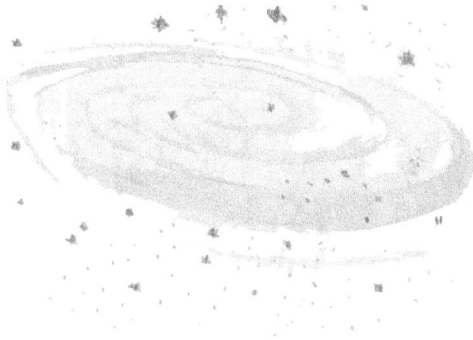

FOUR LETTER WORDS

Four letter words, the vulgar kind, that's what we hear always,
in the most elite of company, or on the street today.

We hear them on the radio and on the TV too,
most folks seem to think it's quite the thing to do.

The movies they all do them that's what we want, they say,
so they really turn them in the wildest kind of way.

When I was young they told me anyone who used them was a dope
I thought I'd try them one day, so they washed my mouth with soap.

Although, I have researched it makes neither sense or rhyme,
that the use of filthy language is the status symbol of our time.

$#!!,

&^$%

@$%*

THOSE DAYS WILL YET LIVE ON

If I had a time machine, I'd travel back once more,
to those carefree days of childhood in those long gone days of yore.

I'd live again those memories beneath the old oak tree,
listening to the crickets chirrup and the buzzing of the bee.

I'd walk down through the meadow to sit on a fallen log,
and hear again the serenade of an amorous fat bullfrog.

While the smaller frogs around him joined in the chorus too,
extending a happy welcome to a season fresh and new.

I'd lie again on a grassy knoll and watch the clouds go by,
wafted along by the breezes across the dome of the sky.

Darting swiftly in and out like children up there on high,
playing tag or follow the leader as they go rushing by.

I'd sit again on Grandma's knee while she, a story told,
or read one from the Bible and its wonders did unfold.

I know I can't return again to an hour long past gone,
but ever in my memory, those days will yet live on.

SPRINGTIME IN THE MOUNTAINS

In spring my heart yearns for the mountains
for those peaks rearing up lofty high,
where billowing mists form a halo
way up near the blue of the sky.

Once again o'er her slopes I'd go roaming
or pause by a pool clear and deep,
to search for the first blue violets
waking up from the long winter's sleep.

The scent of arbutus and laurel
from some glen rising up through the trees,
would sweeten the air with its fragrance
as it's carried along by the breeze.

I'd listen again to the cataract's fall
as it comes sweeping down with a roar,
then burbles and sings as it ambles along
on its way to some more peaceful shore.

All of her sounds are like music
some rolling, some thunderous, some soft,
some hushed as the pines quiet whisper
when the wind waves its branches aloft.

In spring my heart yearns for the mountain
to stand as in days gone so long,
again, enthralled by the wonder
of her beauty, her perfume, and song.

THE GIFT OF TIME

Each year we live is a bonus
after our three score and ten,
an extension from the heavenly Father
of the days we shall spend among men.

A gift for our enjoyment
or more time for the tasks we delay,
and seem to ever save for tomorrow
rather than perform them today.

If I had another lifetime
if I had another day,
how sad to face the judgment,
with only this to say.

THE PRIVILEGE OF CHOICE

Like a bit of lint
carried along by the breeze,
or a leaf moving on
through some windswept trees.

So flows our life swiftly
relentlessly passing by,
from the day we are born
until the day we die.

Though we can never alter
its ongoing flow,
we can each choose the channel
in which it shall go.

LIVE IN THE Present.

BIRDS OR PEOPLE

I watch the birds that congregate around the feeder in my tree,
some are quiet and peaceful, some aggressive as can be.

Some sit quietly and eat, content their food to share,
with all the other birds that are gathered there.

But some don't seem to care about the others of their kind,
their greedy hearts won't let them have a caring kind of mind.

They feud and fuss and chatter and drive the other birds away,
then there is no way possible they could eat it all today.

As I sit and watch them, one thing's quite clear to me,
just how much like people these little feathered creatures be.

A THOUGHT FOR THE NEW YEAR--1969

From the earliest dawn of history, the moon high in the sky,
has been thought about with romance by lovers far and nigh.

She seemed a thing of mystery, so pale and far away,
so very unattainable to fade with light of day.

Some have called her Luna, a goddess bright and gay,
to whom they offered homage for her light upon their way.

Farmers used her phases to plant their crops down here,
and ensure a bounteous harvest at the ending of the year.

Some saw a green and ghostly thing of cheese of palest hue,
and thought she faded quite away and then she started new.

Some said a man lurked in her depth although she was quite fair,
and if you looked so closely, you thought you saw him there.

Now things are very different since our astronauts did go,
and said way out beyond her, that her secrets they might know.

We saw them bravely sail away with apprehensions sore,
then saw their swift and safe return to earth's firm and stable shore.

They say she's but a lump of rock all covered o'er with grime,
and marked with many craters by the meteors through time.

I wonder what we've gained or lost since this costly look,
once the moon influenced our lives, not just our pocketbooks.

BEAUTY THAT SWIFTLY PASSES

We look for beauty on a hillside,
aglow with the shades of fall,
or a lovely splash of color
along the side of a garden wall.

But they oft last only a moment
in the span of a busy day,
like the flash of a tiny hummingbird
as he passes by on his way.

Or perhaps a shining cobweb
covered with morning dew,
as it sparkles like bits of silver
on a morning fresh and new.

Sometimes it's just a rainbow
or a butterfly's colorful wing,
gliding lazily along
in the early days of Spring.

Or a golden ray of sunshine
peeping over a mountain crest,
or a sky lit up with color
as the sun sinks in the West.

Don't rush too fast to view them
in the course of your busy day,
for soon they will just be history,
lost in the pages of yesterday.

A SNAKE'S VIEW OF LIFE

The way that I see it
through the eyes of a snake,
no one seems to care
if I never get a break.

Some folks think a snake
is just seeking a time,
to bite someone
without reason or rhyme.

A crawly creature
of evil you see,
that should never be allowed
to roam around free.

Because I lived in the garden too,
and was fooled by Satan,
just like you.

You knew what God said,
a fact that's quite true,
but He never told me
what I should not do.

Satan told me when God said you would die,
he either was kidding
or told a big lie.

All I am doing
is protecting my head,
when you come along
and step on my bed.

Just let me seek some food,
if I get hungry today,
I won't ever bite you
if you don't get in my way.

I'll catch all the rodents
that infest your house,
whether it be a big fat rat
or a small, tasty mouse.

Then I'll find a snug place
to rest and to hide,
when the north winds blow
and it's cold outside.

Let me live my life
the best way that I can,
for really I am not
the great enemy of man.

ALL ABOUT RABBITS

If you want to learn about the rabbit
just read this tale of mine,
there's a bit of education
in almost every line.

I thought they laid bright-colored eggs
when I was very small,
but then I learned it was just a tale
that was taller than tall.

They live in all countries
some even in town,
but if you want to catch one
you'll have to chase it down.

They come in all shades
O white, brown and gray,
I even saw a pink one
in a store one day.

Some folks call them rabbits
some call them hares,
some call them bunnies
but really who cares.

They're soft and fluffy
with tails, short and round,
and the cutest bit ears
that can ever be found.

If you try to count them
as they come hopping past,
you'll have to be quite speedy
they multiply so fast.

And if you want to buy one
to enjoy the cheer it brings,
you better watch it closely,
or your house will be filled with the things.

WHERE EAGLES FLY

You can live your life on the lowest plane
as a pig within a sty,
or you can rise and spread your wings to soar
up where the eagles fly.

Once God sent his precious Son
to live in this world of sin,
to teach us it was possible
a more free and joyous life to win.

Then He shed His blood on a lonely hill
the awful price to pay,
to redeem us back from Satan's grasp
and show us a better way.

Why live down here on the lowest plain
in this world of sin and strife,
when you can rise above it all
to live an abundant life.

You don't have to wait for a better day
in a land beyond the sky,
you can spread your wings today to soar
up where the eagles fly.

GIFT OF LAUGHTER

The gift of laughter is a thing
that should be prized by all,
by the king within his palace
or the peasant, humble and small.

Wise men have called it medicine
to ease man's gravest ill,
to chase away the shadows
that would ensnare his will.

When pain would hold you captive
just a thought of laughter brings,
the strength to break its shackles
that your spirit may take wings.

If you have this gift of laughter
as a deep and lasting part,
it will give you, though old in body
a young and merry heart.

THE LEGEND OF THE WHISPERING TREE

Let me tell you about the white pine
a very special tree,
with long and slender needles
in the mountains of Tennessee.

It takes on a silver glow
as it reflects the sun's bright light,
and birds roost in its dense branches
to protect them in the night.

If you sit beneath it
on a gentle, breezy day,
it seems to sing and whisper
as its branches bend and sway.

They say the spirit of the Indians,
that once dwelt beside this tree,
forever sighs and whispers
of a terrible tragedy.

When they once were driven
by the white man's cruel hand,
and made to dwell forever
in a strange and different land.

Never more to see the hills
where they once roamed free,
and that is why they call it
the whispering tree.

This is just a legend
that in youth was told to me,
about the whispering white pine
and the fate of the Cherokee.

JUST MUSING ABOUT THE LONG-GONE PAST

People today can't imagine
how we lived in days of old,
because we had few earthly possessions
they think we must have had misery untold.

At a time when men made the living
and women cared for children and home,
when marriage lasted a lifetime
and a spouse didn't wander or roam.

When there was time to visit with neighbors
and friends came often to call,
because there were no televisions
and nowhere to visit a mall.

I just want to let folks know
we didn't live in misery,
we had many kinds of entertainment
and many beautiful things to see.

There were books and magazines to read
newspapers, with comics too,
we had spelling bees and quiltings
and singings, quite a few.

We played games, like spin the bottle,
or sometimes did charades,
we even played some card games
like rook or perhaps, old maids.

I could continue on and on
a fact that is quite true,
about the many fun things
we had back then to do.

But I don't want to bore you
so, I'll just shorten this rhyme,
and tell you more about it
at a more convenient time.

THE WORLD'S MOST PROFOUND MYSTERY

Why men spend so much time preparing
to meet God after they die,
when they can walk hand in hand with Him
through all of their life, here and hereafter.

When I have finished my journey on earth
and my friends are all gathered nigh,
to speak of my faults and my failures
or my virtues to laud with a sigh.

If to speak of my assets and values
find only some small words they should,
let it be this I pray Lord,
She went about doing good.

TRADITIONS

There is no one infallible
among the human race,
who never makes an error
at any time or place.

None can read God's truth so clear
even in His Holy Book,
that there's not one smallest error
to cloud its brightness up.

Once to Israel alone
God gave the truth aright,
but soon her many errors
made dim, its crystal light.

She hear the call of pride and power
along tradition's way,
'til God's pure truth was hidden
and darkness ruled the day.

He came to dwell among them
as prophets oft' foretold,
the time, the place, the circumstance
in words to plain and bold.

Yet to their heart no word of truth
could penetrate and so,
they crucified their promised one
two thousand years ago.

I often wonder if today
our Lord should come, as then,
to point out truth and wisdom
to the erring sons of men.

They would not mock and scorn Him
drive the nails just as before,
because pride and power had led them
in traditions way once more

Tradition is an evil god
and how he shouts with glee,
when he can lure the foolish ones like you, and you and me.

O NATION MINE

Awake! Arise! O nation mine
from out your lethargy,
Arise! Stand up before the world
fulfill your destiny.

Tis carved in stone of liberty
within your law, tis writ,
tis even stamped upon your coin
each precept echoes it.

That God is here the ruler
that we his people be,
just as Israel of old
Oh! Why can you not see.

That all the world is mocking
at intolerance and hate,
at our every injustice
be it small or very great.

At our youth, debauched by alcohol
our highways drenched with blood,
at the dope and marijuana
that engulf us as a flood.

At the crime and moral laxness
that abounds on every hand,
through each city, town and hamlet
of this proud and mighty land.

At the way we smear each other
using varied lies and tricks,
just to get a man elected
in the name of politics.

At our many lofty idols
looming dark against the sky,
making dim God's brightness
to a word that's passing by.

These things base and so unworthy
make Him bow his head in shame,
while a proud and careless people
bring dishonor to His name.

Can you not hear an echo
from the history of the past,
the sound of mighty empires
crashing down to ruin, at last.

Awake! Arise! O nation mine
before it's e'er too late,
and with the nations that forgot him
God forever, seals your fate.

THERE IS ONLY TODAY;
TOMORROW NEVER COMES

The past is all behind us
and ever shall remain,
tis only in the present
that we count our loss or gain.

Each morn, a page that's clean and white,
each night a record true,
that's writ within the Book of Life,
of all we say or do.

Tomorrow never comes, you know,
tho seek it if we should,
we'd only find today again
your work both ill and good.

The future, God holds in His hand,
the past we can't reclaim,
yet He has given us today
to use our feeble flame.

To light a beacon, strong and bright,
to guide some pilgrims ore,
who'll walk the same dark road
we've trod so many years before.

LOVE THAT IS REAL

Some think that love is a fragile thing,
as flowers that bloom in earliest spring.

That if you don't cultivate and tend it each day,
like the flowers of springtime, it will soon fade away.

But love that is real is of a sturdier kind,
a gift from the Father, human hearts to bind.

It keeps on giving from day to day,
and we know that it never will vanish away.

If someone should ask me great love to explain,
I would give them the answer in words, simple and plain.

Great love is compassion, it's a kind, helping hand,
to soothe someone's anguish or to help them to stand.

It's an extension of self to supply someone's need,
to strengthen the weary or the hungry to feed.

It's patience when we would more hurriedly go,
but other feet are more plodding and slow.

It's a feeling of joy when another is praised
although they're just following a trail that we blazed.

Great love knows no envy, it's never jealous or unkind,
and if we research it, there's one thing we will find.

That the proof of our love is in the deeds done each day
not in the things that we think or the words that we say.

TODAY IS ALL YOU CAN CLAIM AS YOUR OWN

I viewed the past with a trouble heart
and it robbed me of my joy,
just as when in childhood
I wept for a broken toy.

I tried to view the future
to see what was in store,
but all I found was a troubled mind and loss of joy
just as I found before.

Then a voice came to me
from the depths of my troubled mind,
you'll never find true happiness
until you leave the past behind.

And trust the distant future
to hands that are strong and sure,
to guide you in their loving way
to the tings that will endure.

Live each day as it comes to you
with a happy thankful heart,
it is all you can ever claim as your own
of time's swiftly passing part.

And let your cup of joy o'er flow
and reach out to some passing soul,
to lift their broken spirit
and make their happiness your goal.

Then I'll pour my boundless blessings
into your cup each day,
and you'll find the joy of living
in a new and better way.

That neither past nor future
can steal your peace away,
If you stop your constant striving
and live only in today.

LIVE IN THE Present.

FOR OUR CENTENNIAL CELEBRATION

There were no spires
reaching up to the sky,
no chimes or bells
in steeple so high.

It was just a small building
in woodland away,
that our forefathers erected
and came there to pray.

The people were sincere
and honest and plain,
all of them labored
with little of gain.

And there at the altar
of this humble place,
they found courage
and help all life's trials to face.

It was rustic and rugged
in earlier days,
but its walls often echoed
with worship and praise.

Now we've enlarged it
and made it quite neat,
gave it soft flowing music
and a comfortable seat.

We no longer labor
with little of gain,
but inside we're still sincere
and honest and plain.

And to this same altar
we still find our way,
to meet with each other
to worship and pray.

And here we find strength
and courage as they,
to conquer the trials we meet
on life's way

OLD LANDMARKS

Some folks would erase the old landmarks
and replace them with things that are new,
although they yet remain useful
their structures still standing and true.

Some folks would erase the old Bible
with its precepts so shining and bright,
and replace it with books that would lead us
into realms of darkness and night.

Why do we stand by and watch them
make mockery of all that is right?
Do we fear we might soil our garments
if we dared to join in the fight?

Come on! Speak up all the people
who knows that old Bible is true,
don't let it be lost by the wayside
Come! Make your pledges anew.

Come on! Put on all your armor
then go out and join in the fray,
don't let the forces of evil
destroy its teachings today.

FOUR SCORE YEARS

Four score years seems a very long time
to someone who twenty will be,
but it passes on wings as swift as the wind
or as waves rolling out to sea.

Time waits for no one,
so do today what your mission may be.
if you continue to wait for tomorrow,
it will never be finished you see.

If there's a kind word that needs to be spoken
or the call to share someone's pain.
take time for an opportunity
once it's gone, will never be again.

EVOLUTION

A play on words, a classic pun,
explaining the mystery of how life on earth begun.

Two bits of flotsam just happened to meet,
way out on the crest of the ocean deep.

And started a chain of life you see,
that millions of years later became you and me.

Yet some of it out there floating free,
by some stroke of magic became a tree.

That washed upon a sunny shore,
where no kind of life had ever been before.

There it planted its roots and there it grew,
until all the earth was covered with foliage, fresh and new.

Also with bits of grass and flowers,
that soon became a wonderland of sweet scented bowers.

Yet there were no insects or bees to spread the pollen around,
and nothing to enjoy the fruits of the ground.

It's funny to think of insects in the ocean swimming around,
with no nectar to sip or flower to be found.

Yet somehow they grew and flourished you see,
and at last came out to dwell with the tree.

To sip the nectar and spread pollen around,
so forms of life might happen and grow,
to enjoy the fruits of the earth you know.

Then some of this life that had developed so fine,
turned into animals, a new kind of line.

There were mice and elephants and winged creatures galore,
there were apes and chimpanzees and many, many more.

Then some turned into humans, a quite different kind,
with a new kind of blood and superior kind of mind.

Tis an odd thought to think to what lengths man will go,
to prove there's no one greater than him, you know.

But this complicated machine that I call me,
could never have happened by chance, you see.

The plans had to be drawn, the structure carefully laid,
for truly I am strangely and wonderfully made.

YOUR VISION

Your horizon's broad or narrow
as the vision that you see,
it can stretch beyond the desert
or the widest reach of sea.

It can span the highest heaven
unlimited and free,
of four walls, a ceiling
and a floor your boundary can be.

If your mind is small and narrow
you may fence your neighbor out,
if you are weak and fearful
you may hedge yourself about.

But in these limited confines,
you'll walk from day to day,
never knowing the fulfillment
of the broader, freer way.

But if your vast horizon
stretches out both wide and high,
shedding love from God the Father
on all men far and nigh.

You'll bring a little nearer
the promise long foretold,
when men shall stand as brothers
in peace on earth blessed age of gold.

LET US GIVE THANKS

Our forefathers were so thankful on that first Thanksgiving Day
to our heavenly Father for His blessings on their way.

Some simple food, a rustic hut, with hardships yet untold,
a crackling fire and clothing to shield them from the cold.

Also for the Indians, their only neighbors here,
who gave them their friendship and their help throughout the year.

When we think of all the blessings that He doth on us outpour,
and we think that we are due them and reach out for more and more.

Of how our hearts are filled with striving and much discontent,
when we only should be thankful for the blessings He has sent.

So let us pray this prayer together with sincere and honest heart,
that we may learn to be as thankful as the pilgrims at the start.

Lord, teach us how to praise you and to thank you every day,
even for the simple things that come to bless our way.

A golden sky at sunset and eyes with which to see,
the beauty all around us so lavish and yet free.

The sounds of music and laughter and ears to hear it too,
teach us true enjoyment as each day comes in new.

Take away our strivings, let our restless murmurings cease,
that we may learn true contentment as we walk with you in peace.

Give
Thanks

HAVE YOU EVER?

Have you ever walked through a meadow
where the grass grew green and tall?
Have you ever walked in a woodland
in the early days of fall?

Have you ever watched a sunrise
at the dawning of the day?
so very bright and beautiful,
it took your breath away.

Have you ever counted stars at night,
or heard the song of the whippoorwill,
or heard the sounds of katydids,
as their tempo rose and fell?

Or did you say tomorrow,
I'll have another day,
and then keep rushing onward
in that same unbending way?

As I think back to my childhood
to those long gone, carefree days,
to a people much less hurried
with far more simple ways.

They had time to visit neighbors,
to share their cares and joys,
they had time to listen to the prattle
of little girls and boys.

They didn't have a lot of things
as people do today,
but were content and happy
in their quiet and simple way.

Now we scurry here and there,
we run fast to and fro,
we don't take time to smell the flowers
along life's way we go.

The more we get, the more we want,
and on the struggle goes,
until within a casket
at last we find repose.

Too late to smell the flowers,
or watch the stars at night,
too late to see a sunrise
by the early morning's light.

To late to visit neighbors,
or share their cares and joys,
too late to listen to the prattle,
of little girls and boys.

Tis sad to think how much we missed
as fast we hurried on
then found that all our tomorrows
had slipped away and gone.

SPACE, GOD'S DOMAIN

Oh! Man so vain and foolish who far in space would go,
to conquer distant planets, say! Did you not know?

A wise creator made them in the ages gone before,
perhaps, ten thousand years ago, or maybe even more.

He set them all in order, according as He saw,
to move in perfect harmony by strict unbending law.

Then He chose one that was perfect, chose an orbit sure and true,
gave it rich soil, air, and water, and prepared it just for you.

With fish, and fowl and animals and many tiny seed,
for growth and vegetation to supply your every need.

Then He sent it spinning, turning, its mission now begun,
for days and years and seasons on its journey 'round the sun.

He gave you full dominion over land, and sea, and air
overall He had created on this planet, rich and fair.

To build, plant and tend it with wisdom and with care,
that future generations, a more abundant life might share.

You've polluted all its waters, filled its air with smog and grime,
eroded its vast surface by denuding it through time.

Now you reach out to the heavens for another place to dwell,
you leave the earth behind you, that you've used, not wise nor well.

But long ago, God gave you a book to guide your ways,
to give you wise instruction to use through all your days.

He said, "with all its environs, the earth, I give to thee,
but heaven and the heavens, they belong alone to me."

Oh! Vain and faithless steward, who far in space would be,
upon some distant planet, pray tell me, do you see?

Even one among them, though you search both far and nigh,
if it were possible to reach it, would your smallest need supply?

THE WINDS OF WAR

I hear the wind's loud wailing,
I hear the sound of marching feet,
with measured treat and briskly
to the drummer's angry beat.

I hear the sounds of children
caught up in war's dread sway,
I see their suffering faces
in the news most every day.

When I was but a little girl,
the sounds, both far and near,
were of many marching feet
as they tramped off to war.

On distant shores, they fought and won,
'tho spirit bruised and sore,
they vowed that they had ended war
that man would fight no more.

But oh so son, so very soon,
I heard that beat once more,
as their sons were called upon,
and they tramped off to war.

Again they won and marched back home,
but oh the tales they told,
of all the many horrors
their eyes saw there behold.

Again they vowed an end to war
  but yet those drums sound on,
  still their feet keep marching
and the winds continue to moan.

Oh! How I long to see the day
when the drums will sound no more,
  when the earth is bathed in silence
  and no heart is bruised and sore.

When there is no more weeping
  as the talk of peace goes on,
  when the winds no longer rage
and the marching feet have gone.

When our great Redeemer reigneth,
  and all drums of war shall cease,
  and earth at last shall welcome
  in her thousand years of peace.

To Be Continued...